BARRON'S
A BUSINESS
SUCCESS GUIDE

Writing Effective Letters and Memos

By

Arthur H. Bell, Ph.D.
and
Cherie Kester

BARRON'S

All inquiries should be addressed to:
Barron's Educational Series, Inc.
250 Wireless Boulevard
Hauppauge, New York 11788

Library of Congress Catalog Card Number 91-15609

International Standard Book No. 0-8120-4674-9

Library of Congress Cataloging in Publication Data
Bell, Arthur H. (Arthur Henry), 1946–
    Writing effective letters and memos / by Arthur H. Bell and
Cherie Kester.
        p.   cm. —(Barron's business success series)
    ISBN 0-8120-4674-9
    1. Commercial correspondence.   2. Memorandums.   I. Kester,
Cherie. II. Title. III. Series.
HF5721.B483   1991
651.7′4—dc20
                                                            91-15609
                                                            CIP

PRINTED IN THE UNITED STATES OF AMERICA
234   5500   98765432

CONTENTS

PREFACE

Hundreds of writers at all levels of business, industry and government have shared their letter- and memo-writing techniques with us for this book. To them, we express deep appreciation.

Ten corporations in particular helped us understand the day-to-day challenges of effective business writing: Lockheed Corporation, TRW, Price-Waterhouse, Santa Fe, Lucky Stores, Apple Computer, Global Technologies, Bullock's, Countrywide Credit, and CADAM. To the management and employees of these organizations, we extend heartfelt thanks.

A. H. B.
Bethesda, Maryland

C. K.
Tustin, California

INTRODUCTION

Why do business people open a book on letters and memos?

Let's not kid ourselves. It's not because they love to write. Much the opposite, in fact. In recent surveys, managers rank writing as one of their least favorite business activities.

But write they must, both for the company and their own careers. *Harvard Business Review* points to writing and speaking skills as the most important factors for managerial promotion.

So to our mutual purpose. You want a short cut to successful letters and memos. We want to provide that short cut as concisely and painlessly as possible.

Here's how this brief book works. In Chapter 1 (I Like Your Style) we'll put the pretentious guff of bureaucratic language in mothballs. You can learn to write as naturally as you speak, and almost as quickly. Then, in Chapter 2 (Read-Me Layouts), we'll focus on the shape and format of letters and memos—that all-important "look" that communicates professionalism. Chapter 3 (Recipes for Successful Communication) teaches how logical, persuasive patterns of organization can be customized to fit your writing needs.

Remaining chapters lead you through all God's plenty of letter types and memos: good news, bad news, mixed news, informational messages, persuasive communication, and difficult writing tasks.

One last word before we start. In the following pages, we've tried to make every word count. We know that you didn't pick up this book for leisure reading, but instead for practical solutions to writing problems. If you have questions or difficulties as you work with this book, don't hesitate to write to us. We would like nothing better than to help you achieve your writing goals.

Art Bell
Dept. of English
Georgetown University
Washington, DC 20057

I LIKE YOUR STYLE

The Natural Voice for Professional Writing

Most of us in business swim in a sea of poor writing styles.

What is style? The short answer to that question is easy: style is "you" in writing. When you write naturally, you write with style.

The long answer to the question goes like this. Style is the window through which your reader sees what you have to say, your content. When that window is fogged over by dense, bureaucratic language, the reader may fail to see your point entirely. By contrast, a clear, easy style lets your reader look through your words, not at your words. Your intentions and meaning stand out.

STYLES WE LOVE TO HATE

Most of us in business swim in a sea of poor writing styles. The memos, letters, reports, and other communications we receive are often too long, too awkward, and too confusing for their own good.

Take, for example, the memos you receive from the *Bureaucrat*. His style never uses a short word where a long one will do:

> *"In accordance with prevailing company regulations in this regard, it is imperative that managerial*

facilitation pertaining to orientation of new employees be undertaken at all levels of authority."

Say *what*? After reading (or attempting to read) this proclamation, what is a manager supposed to think or do? On the third or fourth reading, the intended meaning may start to appear: "All managers must assist in new employee orientation."

Why didn't the Bureaucrat just say so? Probably because he thinks big words automatically create big thoughts and big importance for those who write them.

Not so. Busy professionals want letters and memos that seek to express, not impress. Few business people have the time or the patience to reread bureaucratic messages in search of the actual message.

A second too-common style is that of the *Windbag*. He latches onto a point like a Rottweiler and won't let go:

"There's a hygienic condition of concern not only to me but to all employees on the fifth floor. For the past several days, to my personal knowledge, and perhaps longer, according to people I've spoken with, the dispenser for paper hand towels next to the sinks in Room 368, the men's room, has remained empty of said towels and is at the present time still in need of refilling."

The problem here is overkill. The Windbag cuts butter with an ax. If the message is simply, "The towel dispenser needs refilling," he should say so.

Finally, there's the style found in letters and memos from the *Hothead*. These are the messages that, *a la* Clint Eastwood, "make your day": the angry, sarcastic, biting words that bring out the worst in every reader:

"Your presentation stunk. I told you NOT to use slides. Didn't you attend my training sessions on public speaking??? Obviously you weren't paying attention!"

3

The style of the Hothead tempts a reader to respond in kind—as demonstrated in the "memo wars" so common in corporations. No style, in fact, is so costly to a company as the Hothead's style. It leads to precipitous actions, poor morale, unnecessary meetings and messages, and even transfers or resignations.

FINDING YOUR OWN STYLE

You know you're not a Bureaucrat, a Windbag, or a Hothead in your business messages. But you may not know who you *are* for writing purposes—what you should sound like, how your messages should appear on paper.

This misunderstanding leads directly to the nightmares of Writer's Block. We've all experienced the agony of false starts (or worse, no start at all) when an important memo or letter has to be written *now*. Or, after a promising beginning, we may hit the wall of Writer's Block halfway through the document. We read what we've written and moan, "This is all wrong. It isn't what I want to say."

At such moments, the culprit isn't lack of knowledge or a limited vocabulary. Writer's Block occurs when we refuse to let ourselves *be* ourselves—be natural—in expressing our message.

Here's a case in point. Cynthia Maxwell recently was promoted to one of the vice president positions of a large Boston bank. "I had to write more," she says, "often in the form of messages directly to the bank president or the board of directors. I experienced an incredible case of verbal constipation. I wanted my writing to sound as prestigious as my new job title. But that kind of writing just wouldn't flow for me. I would begin, then fiddle with each word in the first sentence, then begin all over again."

Cynthia Maxwell rediscovered her own style when the chairman of the board told her, over lunch, that the board valued the K.I.S.S. principle above all others in communication: "Keep It Simple, Stupid!" All the bank president and the board wanted was Cynthia's clear thinking expressed as naturally and concisely as possible.

"Now," Cynthia Maxwell reports, "I imagine myself talking to my reader. That technique helps me get right to my point and say it clearly."

THE ELEMENTS OF A NATURALLY PROFESSIONAL STYLE

Simply describing a desirable writing style doesn't do us much good. Let's say, for example, that we agree that professional writing should be *concise, organized, natural* and *appropriately friendly*. In fact, let's say that you memorized these qualities of style, repeated them to yourself whenever beginning a writing task, and named your children after them (Concisa, Organzus, etc.).

What has changed? Probably nothing. Knowing *about* style is like knowing about running. You have to "just do it," in the words of the Nike ad, to change your actual performance.

Therefore, we'll take time out right now to practice each of the stylistic goals we've defined. Though you may feel a bit like a kid in school again, take out a piece of paper and try the following exercises in style. You can then check your work against the recommended answers at the back of the book. (Come on, *do* these mental push-ups. It only takes a few minutes, and you'll be building your writing power.)

1. Rewrite this windy passage to make it more concise:

"The appointed supervisor with responsibility for approving time schedule variations is Margaret Duncan, and it is to her that all requests for lunch period absences from the workplace for more than one hour and fifteen minutes should be directed for processing and authorization."

Notice, by the way, that real employees would probably pay no attention to this garbled prose.

2. Rewrite these sentences to improve organization.

"New employees should report to their work units no later than 9 a.m. on August 1. They must already have completed the Orientation Course beginning on July 26. No new employee will be admitted to the Orientation Course without health certification, available through Physician's Medical Center beginning July 15. A signed letter of employment must be presented at the time of the medical examination."

New employees could be confused by this organizational spaghetti. What should they do and in what order?

3. Rewrite these sentences so that they sound natural, as if spoken by a human being instead of a robot.

"In my capacity as personnel director, I am authorized to express on behalf of the company the general consensus of approval with regard to your decision to accept our offer of employment."

Would you feel welcomed by this message, or does it communicate just the opposite of its apparent intent?

4. Rewrite these sentences so that they sound appropriately friendly.

"I am in receipt of your resignation letter. After seven years of our close association on several projects, I deem it useful to meet personally to discuss the content of your letter. Therefore, I request that you contact my secretary for an appointment at your earliest convenience."

In your more friendly rewrite of this passage, assume that the resignee's name is Bob. Try to work the name smoothly into your more personable revision.

IN WRITING, WE ARE WHAT WE EAT

Do people really write as awkwardly and obscurely as suggested in passages 1 through 4 above? Decide for yourself by looking through recent communiques from "upstairs" in your company—from your benefits office, from your legal counsel, from your training division, from your professional association, from your engineering staff.

Sadly, we swallow thousands of mischosen, misplaced words every business day. On such a diet, we may forget the pleasure of that rare business morsel: a crisp, clear sentence.

Worse, we may start to dish out the same verbal slop we receive. We receive a one-page memo that should have taken one paragraph, and respond to it in kind with our own page or two of gobbledygook. Not surprisingly, questions arise when the message is misunderstood. Meetings are necessary, as are more messages in writing and by phone. Office staff, along the way, requests over-time to deal with the extra keyboarding, photocopying, and scheduling.

The result? We come to think of corporate life as a stagnant swamp of inaction. We think of ourselves as men-tal mammoths caught in that swamp. And the company wonders why profits are slipping.

You can break the cycle of "garbage in/garbage out" by upscaling your verbal environment during the business day. Subscribe to (and read!) superb business writing, as found in *Fortune, Business Week, Forbes, INC, Working Woman,* and other popular business magazines. For models of specific business documents, build a small office library beginning with this book and also including some of these recommended titles:

Bell, Arthur H. *Business Communication: Toward 2000.* Cincinnati, OH: South-Western, 1991.
Bovee, Courtland L. and John V. Thill. *Business Communication Today,* second edition. New York: Random House, 1989.
Pearce, C. Glenn, Ross Figgins, and Steven P. Golen. *Business Communication: Principles and Applications,* second edition. New York: John Wiley, 1988.

Roman, Kenneth and Joel Raphaelson. *Writing that Works*. New York: Harper & Row, 1987.
Sigband, Norman B. and Arthur H. Bell. *Communication for Management and Business*. New York: Harper Collins, 1988.

By reading at least some good business writing each day, you can strengthen your own ability to write naturally, clearly, and quickly—in short, your ability to write professionally.

CHAPTER 2

"READ ME" LAYOUTS AND CONVENTIONS

Eye Appeal for Persuasion

The medium is the message.

Marshall McLuhan

Try this experiment with the next business letter or memo you receive. Glance at it just for a second or two, then put it aside to answer these two questions:

- Did the message appear to be important? What initial clues revealed the message as either hot stuff or junk mail?
- Did the message appear easy to read or tough sledding? Again, what clues led you to form your early estimate of its readability?

Your very first conclusions about a letter or memo have much to do with a) whether you read the message at all, b) how you look upon the message sender, and c) how you interpret and act upon the message itself.

Consider your probable response to a page filled by one gargantuan paragraph, printed singlespaced, in a too-light dot matrix font. No headings help you focus on highlights; no bullets or numbered lists help you make sense of items in series. You conclude, justifiably, that you don't *want* to read this message. If you must read it, you do so in a negative frame of mind that may influence your perception of, and response to, the message content.

Marshall McLuhan championed a principle important

for every business writer: "The medium is the message." McLuhan points out that the medium of a letter or memo—its form on the page, its length, its printed appearance—is a vital part of the message being communicated.

Take, for example, the book you're now reading. Would it communicate as well to you if you were reading the same words in mimeographed or handwritten form? Publishers and authors know the importance of book design—everything from the book cover to the chosen fonts and line spacing—to make words credible and lively. In the same way, you can design your letters and memos for best effect.

CONTROLLING YOUR MESSAGE LAYOUTS

Particularly if you dictate, you may feel that the ultimate appearance of your message on the page is somewhat out of your control. A secretary or other staff member may routinely decide what document format to use, how long paragraphs will be, and where white space will occur. More than one manager has been ruefully surprised to see, in the final printed verison, how deadly dull a dictated message appears to be.

For successful letters and memos, you must take control of the *printed appearance* of your messages, not just their content. We're not suggesting that you must key in your own documents, although more and more managers find themselves doing just that. You must, however, let secretaries and other staff members know your wishes regarding layout, paragraph length, text placement, font size, headings, and related matters. Whenever possible, make these requirements known before rather than after the document has been typed or word-processed.

In dictating, for example, simply let your secretary know what letter or memo style you want (several styles are described in this chapter); where you want to end paragraphs; where you want a bulleted or numbered list set off by white space on either side; where you want inset margins; and where you want larger or smaller type sizes and different fonts. This added bit of work on your part will pay large dividends in creating effective business messages.

BUSINESS LETTER LAYOUTS

So far in the 1990s, the most common letter layouts (in order) remain the block style, modified block style, and simplified style. Companies and government organizations usually prefer one of these forms over others, or particular forms for specified types of communication. Sears, for example, typically uses block style for letter communication with customers and simplified style for correspondence with suppliers.

Take the preferences and traditions of your organization into consideration when determining which layout to use for your letters. No one style is right or wrong; each has strengths and weaknesses, as explained below, that must be weighed in relation to your purpose and audience.

BLOCK STYLE

This style is used in approximately 70 percent of all business letters, perhaps because it is so easy to teach to office staff. As shown below, all letter elements are placed flush against the left margin. The letter body is placed so that it straddles the middle of the page. For letters longer than one page, the letter text on the final page begins after the top margin and is not centered.

Block style has the advantages of ease of preparation and a brisk, business-like appearance. Some writers feel that its lack of balance on the page (all elements, after all, are pushed to the left) may not be appropriate for more social or persuasive uses of the business letter. You may not want to use block style for readers more familiar with

Example of Block Style

(letterhead centered on page)

March 15, 1991

Ruth Foster, Manager
Conway Construction, Inc.
2983 Western Highway
Cincinnati, OH 60232

Dear Ms. Foster:

Last week you asked me to review letters sent from your company and to recommend a standard letter format for use by your employees.

More than a dozen variations of business letter format appeared in the 200 Conway letters I reviewed. When employees are free to choose or invent their own letter formats, the company suffers in three ways:

- readers look upon nontraditional letter formats as errors
- readers infer a lack of coordination at Conway based on wide variations in letter style
- Conway employees spend extra time converting letters from one format to another when letter texts must be revised.

For general correspondence at Conway, I recommend the block letter style, as described in the enclosed book, *Writing Effective Letters and Memos*. I believe you will find this style helpful in communicating a consistent company image through your correspondence.

Sincerely,

Robert D. Johnson

Robert D. Johnson
Communication Consultant

RDJ/coe

Enclosure: *Writing Effective Letters and Memos*

other styles. These readers include older persons, who grew up with indented forms of letter-writing, and many international readers.

MODIFIED BLOCK STYLE

This style, through the 1960s, was the predominant form for business correspondence. As such, it may remain the expected form for many older business readers. These readers may, in fact, look upon more contemporary styles such as block style and simplified style as relatively cold and routine in nature.

The modified block style is somewhat more difficult to use than block style. The person keying in the letter must locate the horizontal center of the page for the date and signature block. All other letter elements are placed against the left margin. In one popular variation of the modified block style, paragraphs are indented five spaces.

For some readers, the modified block style looks more balanced on the page and therefore more gracious or social in appearance. The modified block style is commonly used for correspondence between executive levels of management and for persuasive letters such as sales and proposal correspondence.

SIMPLIFIED STYLE

This final style is used in no more than 10 percent of all business correspondence. As is apparent in the following example, the simplified style streamlines the business letter to emphasize content over more personal or complimentary aspects of the letter.

In placement on the page, the simplified style abides by the same rules as block style. All letter elements are placed against the left margin. Notice, however, that the salutation and complimentary close found in block style are missing entirely in the simplified style.

Obviously the simplified style is not the style of choice

Example of Modifed Block Style

(letterhead centered)

March 15, 1991

Mr. Herbert Reed, Director
Southern States Charities, Inc.
3923 Lee St.
Savannah, GA 29832

Dear Mr. Reed:

Thank you for your letter of March 8 in which you inquire
about appropriate letter formats for use in your solicitation
letters.

Although the block style is used for most business communications, I recommend a less common form—modified
block style—as particularly suited to your use. Unlike letter
elements in block style, the various parts of a modified block
letter are balanced on the page. This more traditional "look"
may strike your mature readership as more professional and
less stark.

The modified block style is explained in the enclosed book,
Writing Effective Letters and Memos. Please don't hesitate
to contact me if I can be of further assistance.

                                Sincerely,

                                Robert D. Johnson

                                Robert D. Johnson
                                Communication Consultant

RDJ/coe

Enclosure: *Writing Effective Letters and Memos*

for correspondence in which interpersonal warmth and formal politeness are high priorities. But in routine or mass-processed mailings, the simplified style saves the reader and the writer time by getting right to the main message without preliminary courtesies.

This is not to say that the simplified style is (or has a right to be) inevitably impersonal. As in the example below, the reader's name can be worked smoothly into

---

Example of Simplified Style

(letterhead centered)

March 15, 1991

Pat Connors, Accounts Supervisor
Acme Training Supplies, Inc.
22 Richfield Plaza
Dallas, TX 29832

REQUEST FOR RECEIPT OF PAYMENT

In my last order for seminar materials, Pat, I neglected to request your receipt for my check to Acme dated Feb. 1, 1991 (no. 2382). The check has already cleared, but I need your verification of payment for tax purposes.

I understand that Acme plans to represent a number of business film producers beginning in late 1991. As soon as you know which film titles you will be offering, I would appreciate receiving a price list for purchase or rental.

I've valued our business association over the years. Thanks for your early attention to the receipt request.

Robert D. Johnson

ROBERT D. JOHNSON,
COMMUNICATION CONSULTANT

---

the opening sentences of the letter, serving the purpose of a traditional salutation. Note in this regard that the simplified style lets the writer avoid the problem of deciding between "Mr." or "Ms." for gender-ambiguous names such as Pat and Chris.

In the same way, an expression of well-wishing in the last sentence of the letter can take the place of the complimentary close.

OTHER LETTER ELEMENTS

No matter what letter format you choose, you will probably have occasion to use one or more of the following additional elements. More, however, is not better. Use only those elements that are necessary for your complete business message.

The Attention Line

At times, you may be writing a company without knowing the name of the person who will be reading the letter. In such cases, use an attention line to direct your letter to the intended reader:

> Victory Toys, Inc.
> 892 Jones Road
> Westwood, CA 89232
>
> Attention: Customer Service

The Reference Line

Many government organizations and some corporations expect that reference will be made at the outset of a letter to previous correspondence identified by code number or date. The reference line is usually placed after the inside address or, if an attention line occupies that position, under the date:

John Frederick, Manager
Wilson Autonetics, Inc.
19 Federal Hwy.
Seattle, WA 89232

Reference: your letter, May 17, 1991

(or)

Reference: letter #89A42

The Subject Line

As an aid to orienting the reader to the central message of a letter, a subject line is often placed just before or after the salutation. The use of this letter element lends a somewhat formal or official tone to the letter, and therefore is often omitted in more sociable or persuasive business correspondence.

Joan Trent, Vice President
Reynolds Industries
892 Henderson Dr.
Las Vegas, NV 29832

SUBJECT: 1991 OSHA Revisions

Dear Ms. Trent:

(or)

Joan Trent, Vice President
Reynolds Industries
892 Henderson Dr.
Las Vegas, NV 29832

Dear Ms. Trent:

SUBJECT: 1991 OSHA Revisions

The Salutation

One common problem in completing the salutation occurs when the gender of the addressee isn't known. Don't guess with regard to "Mr. or Ms." when addressing letters to people with gender-ambiguous names (Pat, Chris, Dale, and so forth). Make an effort to determine gender by calling the person's company operator or secretary. Failing that, address the person in the salutation by their full name or by their job title and last name:

Dear Pat Connors:

Dear Supervisor Connors:

"Ms." should be used in the salutation to address all women except those who had indicated a preference, in their correspondence to you or other contact, for "Mrs." or "Miss."

The Complimentary Close

Choosing the appropriate word to precede your signature should be a matter of strategy, not habit. Many business writers use the standby "Sincerely" (a perfectly appropriate complimentary close) long after their business relationship with their reader has warmed to the point of deserving warmer words:

- Regards,
- Best regards,
- Best wishes,
- With best wishes,
- All best wishes,
- Cordially,

You must be the judge to determine when these words can appropriately take the place of "Sincerely." Certainly if you address your reader by his or her first name in the salutation you can maintain the same friendly tone by a warm complimentary close.

Your Signature

Sign your letter with your usual business signature, even though it may differ from your professional name as typed beneath your signature. As a general rule, if you have addressed your reader by his or her first name in the salutation, sign the letter with your first name.

Sincerely,

Thomas R. Smith

With best regards,

Thomas R. Smith

The Reference Initials

Following the signature block, the author of a letter indicates his or her initials in capital letters without periods, then separated by a slash the initials of the letter typist in lower case letters. Alternately, a word-processing code can be used instead of the reference initials. The code indicates where in the company's disk storage system the letter can be found.

Sincerely,

Robert D. Johnson
Communication Consultant

RDJ/coe

or, in place of reference initials or in addition:

WP30A32

The Enclosure Notation

When additional materials are included with the letter, they are named by title (preferably) or by type. This practice helps the person who "stuffs" the envelope make sure that all intended materials have been included. It also helps the recipient of the letter to ask for materials by name in case they were inadvertently left out of the mailing.

Enclosure: "Opportunities in Bond Trading"

or

Enclosure: 1991 company calendar

The cc: and bc: Notations

The cc: notation stands for "carbon copy," a duplication medium used less and less with the advent of photo-copying. The initials continue to be used to preface names of people who have received copies of the letter.

cc: Bob Owens, Linda Valencia, Tom Morgan

The bc: notation stands for blind copy. It appears only on a copy of the letter, not the original. On the copy, it prefaces the names of people who have received a copy of the letter without the knowledge of the recipient of the original letter. Some personnel actions, for example, require that copies of reprimand letters be sent to upper levels of management without notification to the reprimanded employee.

bc: Tracy Wadsworth, Personnel Director

The P.S. (Postscript) Notation

P.S. notations are common in junk mail solicitations, where they are used to highlight special offers or last-minute motivators and calls for action. In other forms of business letters, the P.S. notation should be avoided if at all possible. It signals the inadvertent omission of information from the body of the letter—an omission that can almost always be repaired without a P.S. if the letter is prepared on word-processing.

P.S. I'll be away from my office June 7 through June 19. My assistant, Bob Robbins, will be happy to assist you during this period.

Folding the Letter

Junk mail can usually be recognized by an off-center, sloppy fold. When your business correspondence arrives in a similar condition, the reader's associations are hardly to your advantage.

Take care, therefore, to fold the letter carefully according to one of these traditional procedures:

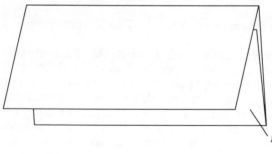

1/2" flap

Note in this fold that a "flap" of approximately ½ inch is left at the bottom of the folded letter to aid the reader in unfolding it.

The French fold is used particularly for window envelopes showing the name and address typed on the letter.

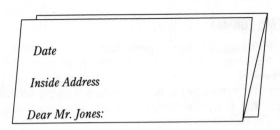

Do not try to fold an 8½″ × 11″ letter to fit into a nonstandard or note-size envelope. Use a business-sized envelope or retype the letter on smaller stationery appropriate for the envelope size.

ENVELOPE CONVENTIONS

A standard-size business envelope is addressed as follows:

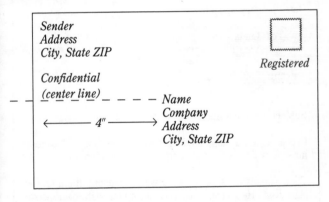

Note that no information is placed lower on the envelope than the ZIP code line for the sake of automatic sorting machines at the post office. Any instructions from the sender such as "Confidential" or "Time-dated Materials" are placed beneath the sender's name and address. Any instructions for the post office such as "Registered" or "Do Not Bend" are placed under the postage.

MEMO FORMAT

Unlike business letters, memos have remained relatively fixed in format over the past decades. Although the order of these elements varies somewhat from company to company, all memos begin with a block specifying (at minimum) the date, the intended reader, the memo writer, and the subject.

In the following sample memo, note that the body text is not centered top to bottom on the page. Many memo writers add their handwritten initials beside their name or at the bottom of the memo.

Sample Memo

Date: January 6, 199___

     To: Linda Evans
           Vice President

  From: Paul Ortega
          Sales Director

Subject: Arrangements for visiting Japanese managers

I've attached a suggested agenda for the twelve Japanese managers who will be visiting our headquarters on Jan. 18.

Their translator, Uko Katama, will accompany them on the plant tour. He will also be available, if you wish, to translate your welcoming speech to the group. It will be helpful for Uko to have a copy of your speech a few days before the visit.

All other arrangements are in order, I believe, for a productive day with these managers. Let's meet briefly on January 17 to handle any last details.

CHAPTER 3

RECIPES FOR SUCCESS

*Quick Plans to
Clarify Your
Writing*

Create a pattern that helps you say all you want to.

Consider various forms of creation. To build a house, a carpenter follows blueprints. For a cake, a baker follows a recipe. Even Nature follows the DNA code. Only the writer frequently insists on "winging it" without a plan when constructing the texts of letters and memos.

You've seen the result too often in your in-basket: disorganized, rambling messages that you must read two or three times to untangle.

And you're not the only one to pay the price for poor planning. The letter or memo writer probably struggled to produce the mess you hold in your hand. It's hard, after all, for a writer who hasn't planned what to do with his or her words to write well.

This chapter suggests five planning aids to benefit both the reader and the writer. These short recipes tell, paragraph by paragraph, how to develop a concise, logical message-text for letters or memos. Like all recipes, of course, these can be varied to suit your individual needs.

HOW TO USE A MESSAGE-TEXT RECIPE

Before considering any recipe to guide your writing, review (out loud, if possible) what it is that you want to communicate. Then, with a firm grasp on your intended message, look over the following recipes. At least one should leap out at you as an ideal step-by-step agenda for writing your message-text.

Or you may find two or more recipes that can be combined to produce an order of ideas that suit your content. Your goal should be to find or create a pattern that helps you say all you want to, no more, no less.

Pattern One — Messages Based on Time

In this pattern, the first paragraph should discuss what has occurred in the past. The second paragraph deals with the present. A final paragraph looks toward the future. In the example below, notice that an initial overview sentence has been added to let the reader know that time will be used to organize the message-text.

Uses: problem descriptions, brief histories, informational summaries with recommendations or forecasts.

Dear Mr. Forest:

As you requested, I've investigated the vandalism problem at Plant #6 for the period 1983 through the present. This letter summarizes my findings, with recommendations. A more detailed report will be forwarded to you early next week.

From the opening of the plant in 1983 through June of 1988, no incidents of vandalism were reported. That summer, however, the company purchased six vacant lots adjoining the plant for employee parking. These lots, it was later discovered, had been used for many years as a baseball and football field for neighborhood youth. From the summer of 1988 through last month, a total of 48 incidents of vandalism have occurred. These range from broken windows in employee automobiles to graffiti on plant walls.

At present, the company's executive council is involved in bi-weekly meetings with neighborhood representatives to resolve the on-going vandalism problem. A total of seven private security guards now assist city police in surveillance and protection of company property.

Looking toward the future, we can predict further outbreaks of vandalism so long as the playground/parking lot issue continues to rankle the neighborhood. I recommend, therefore, that the company assist neighborhood representatives in developing a recreation area for its children. The expense of this worthwhile endeavor will prove to be far less than the costs of an on-going struggle with the neighborhood.

Pattern Two—Messages Based on Space

In this pattern, the first paragraph deals with something at a great distance. The second paragraph focuses on something closer. The final paragraph discusses or describes something right at hand. In the following example, an initial sentence orients the reader to this far-to-near pattern of description.

Uses: informational descriptions, orientations

Dear Ms. Morgan:

We're happy that you will be joining us as a field sales associate. I'm writing to acquaint you in general terms with your regional, community and business park sales territories.

Your sales boundaries extend from Chula Vista on the California/Mexico border to Oceanside, and east as far as El Centro, California. We expect that major clients within this region will be visited at least once every two months as well as on an as-requested basis.

Your home base area is San Diego, where you will probably do 60 to 70 percent of your total volume. In organizing your time, please plan to spend at least two-thirds of your working hours within the city limits of San Diego.

The focal point of your efforts, of course, will be in the Santa Inez Business Park where your office is located. Over 400 potential clients are located within the park, and we know that you will pursue their business aggressively.

Ted Vickers, our Western sales vice president, will meet with you next Wednesday to discuss company goals and sales strategies for your area.

Pattern Three—Messages Based on Changing Perspectives

In this pattern, the first paragraph discusses how you once thought or felt about a subject. The second paragraph describes some crucial event or insight that changed your perspective on the subject. The third paragraph assesses how you now view the subject.

Uses: explanations, analyses, evaluations, personal disclosures, adjustments

Dear Mr. Denton:

When I first read your letter of May 1 regarding a morning traffic problem in front of your home, I will admit to more than a little skepticism. I couldn't imagine how the departure of our company trucks from the Seventh Street lot could block your driveway on Ninth Street, as you describe, for more than an hour each morning.

Two days after receiving your letter, however, I drove to work past your property. There, exactly as you said, were at least ten company trucks lined up at the Ninth Street/ Western Ave. intersection.

The cause, we have since discovered, is a mobile diner located just past that intersection. Drivers were lining up on Ninth Street to buy coffee and doughnuts at the diner before beginning their daily routes. We've talked to the owner of the diner about the traffic problem, and I'm happy to report that he has relocated his operation to Seventh Street, where the line of trucks won't cause a problem.

Thank you for bringing this matter to our attention. We apologize for the inconvenience you've experienced and trust that the problem is now solved.

Pattern Four—Messages Based on Causality

In this pattern, the first paragraph discusses surface symptoms. The second paragraph describes immediate causes of those symptoms. The final paragraph deals with deeper causes.

Uses: personnel evaluations, problem analyses, sales and marketing assessments, trouble reports

Dear Ms. Wenden:

After six successful quarters of sales in the Seattle area, we were both confused by last quarter's results: general sales down 16 percent, on average, across our nine area stores.

As we discussed by phone, some of this downturn can be attributed to layoffs at Boeing, the area's largest employer. During the quarter, Boeing gave layoff notices to approximately 5 percent of its workforce.

But it's dangerous, I believe, to assume that our sales slump is due simply to such layoffs. During the quarter, two powerful competitors—SaveMarts and Bargain Boys—opened a total of eight stores within the greater Seattle area. The grand openings of these stores were accompanied by their heavy advertising of sales items.

I recommend a thorough assessment of the impact of such competition upon our sales.

Pattern Five—Messages Based on Proportion

In this pattern, the first paragraph tells what most people think or feel. The second paragraph focuses on the opinions of a smaller group. The final paragraph discusses the perspective of an even smaller minority.

Uses: meeting and discussion summaries, market descriptions and analyses, personnel and attitudinal evaluations

Dear Mr. Evans:

I have polled company employees on the issue of flexible work scheduling. A total of 308 of the company's 445 employees responded to the survey form included with last month's paychecks.

Most employees (74 percent) favor flex-time based around a core of required hours from 10 a.m. to 3 p.m. Under this plan, an employee could arrange his or her 40 hour week as desired, so long as the core block of required hours is included each workday.

A smaller group (20 percent) wants complete flex-time without the core hours requirement. Many members of this group favor optional Saturday and Sunday working hours for job categories (such as programmers and systems analysts) not usually involved in interdepartmental meetings.

The remainder of those polled (6 percent) were opposed to flex-time entirely. These employees (primarily managers) argue that their work will be made more difficult if employees are allowed to choose their own work schedules.

Based on the result of this thorough poll of employee preferences, I recommend that the company undertake a pilot test of the "core hours" approach to flexible work scheduling.

A FINAL WORD ABOUT RECIPES

No writer likes to be told what to do, even by a helpful recipe. Use these patterns, therefore, to stimulate possibilities for developing your ideas, not as a strait jacket for your imagination. With practice, you will soon find yourself using patterns of thought almost unconsciously. At the same time, you'll find yourself writing much more quickly than ever before.

CHAPTER 4

HERE'S THE GOOD NEWS

*Letters and
Memos That
Say "Yes"*

*What better time to nurture a
good business relationship through
well-chosen words of goodwill!*

At least half of all letters and memos written in business carry good news to the reader: yes, we have the products and services you need; yes, we can fill your order; yes, we can extend credit; yes, we can answer your inquiry; yes, we accept your invitation; yes, we will make an adjustment based on your claim.

The key to successful good news communications lies in using them to build goodwill. Readers are pleased, after all, to receive your "yes" message. What better time to nurture a good business relationship through well-chosen words of goodwill!

THE GOOD NEWS SALES LETTER

Your appropriate enthusiasm for your products or services can be contagious for the reader. There's a fine line, of course, between upbeat enthusiasm and "step-right-up" carnival behavior. Demonstrate the energetic, optimistic spirit of a winner in your sales letters to motivate your reader to say "yes" to your sales appeal.

Notice in the following "before" and "after" examples how the Good News tone increases the power and potential of the sales letter.

Version One: A Lackluster Sales Letter Without the Good News Tone

Dear Mr. Frank:

Since 1984, Union Tire Company has served the tire needs of this community.

During the entire month of May we are offering fleet managers a 15 percent discount on all tires and mounting/balancing charges.

To schedule appointments for your vehicles, please call Jeff Edwards, Service Manager, at 982-3892. Thank you.

Sincerely,

Tony Agnotti

Tony Agnotti
Sales Representative

Version Two: A Lively Sales Letter Employing the Good News Tone

Dear Mr. Frank:

At our lunch together last month, you asked me to let you know right away about any special promotions that could save you hundreds of dollars on tire replacements for your fleet.

I'm happy to send you this advance notice of Union Tire's May sale for fleet managers. We're offering a full 15 percent off all tires, including mounting and balancing charges.

I'll call you tomorrow to answer any questions you have about these discounted prices. With the green light from you, I will be glad to help you schedule your vehicles for installation of great tires at great prices.

With best regards,

Tony Agnotti

Tony Agnotti
Sales Representative

The point in these comparison letters is to remember the good news dimension of every sales letter. The product or service you are offering should be presented as a welcome answer to the client's need. As the sales person, you can feel good about serving those needs—and your good feelings about yourself, your client, and your products or services should shine through in the tone of your sales letter.

GOOD NEWS AND GOODWILL IN ROUTINE RESPONSES

In saying "yes" to a customer order or request, you have an ideal opportunity to build the kind of goodwill that promotes future business. Notice in the following letter to a new customer that the good news (the "yes" message) is followed by a bit of appropriate salesmanship for the company.

Dear Mr. Cort:

Welcome to the Trevex wholesale outlet for more than 1000 floral retailers. Your order, No. 2983, has been filled and will be delivered at your store on March 23 by 12 noon.

We will do whatever we can to deserve your continued business. Don't hesitate to call our customer hotline, (800) 986-9823, with any questions or concerns you have about billings, shipments, or special promotions.

To say thanks for your first order, I've enclosed a 10 percent discount certificate toward your next purchase totalling $800 or more. I've also sent along our Summer catalog, with five "best buys" specials highlighted for your interest.

Best regards,

Lisa Browne

Lisa Browne
Sales Director

In the following response to an inquiry, the writer turns a "win" for the reader (who receives the answer to a question) into a simultaneous "win" for the company by promoting goodwill.

Dear Ms. Underwood:

We were pleased to receive your inquiry (Jan. 2, 1991) regarding the propulsion specifications of the Z70 rocket engine manufactured by this company. Although some aspects of the engine design must remain classified, I have enclosed an engineering fact-sheet providing the thrust data you seek for your thesis.

You may also be interested in viewing "Toward the Stars," a PBS production co-sponsored by Space Design, Inc. This program, scheduled for airing on Feb. 5, reviews the history of rocket technology and discusses many of the issues you mention in your letter. If you can't see it in your area, please contact me and I'll provide a videotape of the program on loan.

Thank you for your interest in our work and products at Space Design, Inc., and best wishes for success in your graduate studies.

Sincerely,

THOMAS B. WATSON

Thomas B. Watson
Public and Corporate Relations

The extra effort toward goodwill in the second and third paragraphs of this letter pays dividends for the company in several ways: one more member of the public is positively impressed by the company, a graduate student may well be attracted to apply to the company in the future for work, and the company's public service efforts via public television receive a bit of advertising.

In this credit communication, the good news of approval sets the stage for some direct marketing of specific products.

Dear Mr. Richmond:

Lindbay Furniture Manufacturing is pleased to approve your revolving credit account #29832 in the amount you requested, $10,000. No interest will be charged on balances paid within 30 days of purchase. A sliding interest amount, as described in the enclosed credit disclosure, will be charged on balances exceeding 30 days.

With summer just a few months away, I'd like you to know about Lindbay's upcoming sale on its popular line of patio furniture March 10–15. Orders received for patio items during this period will receive a 10 percent discount. The enclosed catalog provides details on the patio line and convenient order forms.

We look forward to hearing from you and, again, our sincere welcome as a new Lindbay client.

Cordially,

Roberta Johnston

Roberta Johnston
Customer Representative

SUMMARY KEYS TO DELIVERING GOOD NEWS MESSAGES

1. Show the kind of enthusiasm for your product or service that you want your reader to feel.
2. Present your sales message as a "good news" solution to the reader's needs or problems.
3. Build goodwill for your company by including well-wishing, expressions of appreciation, and other courtesies in even the most routine communications.

CHAPTER 5

HERE'S THE BAD NEWS

*Letters and
Memos That
Say "No"*

Saying "no" takes character.

You'll say "no" in business messages at least as often as you say "yes." Boss, can I have a raise? No, not this quarter. Can your company donate a pickup truck to the Boys Club? No, I'm sorry that we can't. Mr. Manager, I demand compensation for my mental anguish when your product failed. No, we aren't able to grant your claim.

Saying "no" takes character. You're risking angry reactions from those you refuse. They may dislike you—and tell you so to your face. They may talk about you behind your back, or send complaints to your superiors. They may take their business elsewhere.

For these reasons, some managers and other professionals have real trouble communicating bad news. They avoid such confrontations or delegate them to others: "Uh, Ms. Jones, would you take Mitchell aside and explain to him why I can't give him an extra week of vacation. You two seem to be friends." Or they try to disguise every bad news message as neutral or good news: "Mitchell, I'm going to get your input from now on when I draw up the vacation schedule."

The hard truth about bad news is that people will be disappointed. People may get angry. People may blame you. "Heavy lies the head," says Shakespeare, "that wears the crown." Part of the burden of leadership at any level is the necessity of occasionally communicating bad news.

But people prefer honest bad news to dishonest soft-soaping or manipulation. In asking for a price break, for example, a customer would rather receive a courteous turndown than an interminable series of lame excuses: "Well, if it were up to me, I would say yes, but I have to check with Mr. Allen, and he's out of town for several days. In fact, I'm not sure when he will be returning . . ."

This kind of stalling and waffling is business coward-ice, not kindness. Customers and employees understand the fact that you have standards and limitations you must live by. They respect you when you're forthright about what you can and can't do. They resent being conned.

CONVEYING BAD NEWS WITH CONSIDERATE BUFFERS

On many business occasions, you will be able to buffer your delivery of bad news by helpful comments and explanations. For example, colleges tell many scholarship applicants the bad news of "no money" using this type of buffer:

> *"This year State University received more than 4700 applications for the 800 tuition scholarships available. Because of such limited funding, many highly qualified applicants did not receive scholarship aid."*

The letter goes on to deliver the bad news regarding the reader's application and to offer alternative sources for college support.

A Silicon Valley computer company regularly uses this buffer to begin bad news letters to unsuccessful job applicants:

> *"We deeply appreciate your interest in employment at XYZ Corporation. At present, we do not have career openings suitable for your qualifications."*

The letter goes on to say that application materials will be kept on file for a period of one year. Introductory buffers should be informational or complimentary in tone, but never so rosy in tone as to arouse false expectations for the reader. A job applicant, for example, shouldn't be teased with the opening sentence, "Your qualifications are ideal!" if the next sentence conveys the bad news that the job went to someone else.

Here are four useful buffers for a variety of bad news communications.

1. This buffer helps the candidate understand why he or she was not chosen:

> *The company limited its search to candidates with LISP and COBOL programming experience.*

2. This buffer helps late applicants understand why their bids were unsuccessful:

> *The Federal funding cycle required that we arrange subcontractors no later than April 1.*

3. This buffer helps candidates understand their chances:

> *Competition for these three positions was keen. More than 300 applications were received.*

4. This buffer helps an employee feel that his or her contribution was not ignored, even though a raise wasn't forthcoming:

> *Our decisions on merit raises this year were made extremely difficult by the limited funds available. Not all meritorious employees could be recognized by raises.*

CONVEYING BAD NEWS WITHOUT EXTENSIVE EXPLANATION

At times, you may not want or be able to provide cogent justification or explanation for the bad news you deliver.

In credit refusals, for example, you may risk libel action by attempting to specify exactly why credit was denied. Compare, for example, the hazardous explanations in the "before" letter with the safe, brief "no" communication in the "after" version.

"Before" revision:

Dear Mr. Reynolds:

Your application for credit cannot be approved at this time because of substantial unpaid balances on three credit cards; lingering credit problems due to your recent divorce; disputed billings with two department stores; and a low rating of "2" on our measurement scale of employment stability.

This kind of letter is sure to draw angry response and perhaps legal challenge from the reader.

"After" revision:

Dear Mr. Reynolds:

Thank you for applying for credit with XYZ Company. We regret that we cannot extend the credit you request at this time. If you have questions about your credit record, you may contact TRW Credit Services at 982-3892 within 60 days of this letter for a copy of your credit report without charge.

Similarly, you may not choose to cite chapter-and-verse reasons for bad-news responses to many requests and invitations.

Dear Ms. Collins:

I'm sorry to write that I won't be able to accept your kind invitation to present the keynote address for this year's Community Fund convention.

Thank you for thinking of me, and my very best wishes for the success of your meeting.

This kind of direct, polite refusal is preferable to the white lies that so often accompany "no" messages. The writer could have told Ms. Collins, contrary to fact, that he had to be out of town on the convention weekend. If it is later discovered (as it may be) that he has lied, both he and Ms. Collins will feel the awkwardness of the situation. Besides, whether he's caught or not, it's both wrong and unnecessary to lie.

Here's another example of a bad news message without extended explanation, this time in memo form.

To: Virginia Flores
Human Services

From: Brenda Nathanson
Vice President

Subject: Additional Staff

Virginia, I gave careful attention to your well-reasoned request for two additional secretaries. Unfortunately, the budget won't allow me to say yes this year.

Let's get together if you would like to talk about ways to deal with your work load under present staffing limits. I won't forget your request, by the way, when fiscal pressures ease up.

Notice in this memo that the vice president does not choose to give her employee a close justification for her decision. The decision is "no," though delivered politely and with the offer of help.

Especially in decisions regarding new product development, regulatory problems, taxation, personnel, compensation, hiring, and policy, business leaders often find that "less is more"—the less said, the better. This general guideline should not be taken as a license for managers to deny information to clients, employees, and the public. But managers should not feel under the obligation always to supply complete rationales for every "no" decision. The pace and nature of daily business life often make such disclosure both impractical and inadvisable.

BAD NEWS RESPONSES TO CLAIMS

Contrary to the old saying, customers aren't always right. Often they make claims upon the company that cannot and should not be granted.

Take the case of an Ohio bus company. It purchased three commuter-size buses from the manufacturer, Regent Coaches. Within a year, the cloth upholstery in all three buses was showing significant wear. The bus company wrote to the manufacturer to demand that all seat covers be replaced in a more durable material without expense to the purchaser.

From the perspective of the manufacturer, this claim can't be granted. First, seat coverings—along with wiper blades, batteries, and headlight bulbs—are explicitly exempted from warranties on the buses in question. Second, the purchaser selected the least expensive seat-cover fabric (identified in writing by the manufacturer at the time of sale as suitable for "light use" only) even though the buses received heavy daily use.

If possible, the bad news to the purchaser must be delivered in a constructive, nonadversarial way. The manufacturer doesn't want to drive former customers away. For this reason, the following letter suggests options that help the purchaser resolve the seat-cover problem without compromising the warranty standards and policies of the manufacturer.

Dear Mr. Green:

Thank you for your careful description in your May 1 letter of wear-and-tear problems with seat coverings in your Regent buses. Although fabric repairs are exempted from the bus warranty (see paragaph 9), let me suggest a long-term solution to the problem you describe.

The success of your bus routes is amply demonstrated by your number of passengers per day—heavy use you may not have anticipated when you selected fabric for your bus seats. To plan for continued heavy use in the future, you should consider installing DurEver coverings, which do carry a five-year guarantee against tears, fraying, or surface wear.

We can arrange to have these coverings installed on an overnight basis at your site. Costs for your three Regent buses are enclosed on a separate estimate form. Please note that the cost of this upgrade is far less over five years than the two or more sets of cloth seat fabrics you could expect to install in that period.

I'll call you within the next few days to discuss your seat-cover options. Or, if you wish, give me a call at 382-3902.

Sincerely,

Corey L. Watkins

Corey L. Watkins
Service Manager

Will the customer not only swallow the bad news that he isn't getting new seat covers, but also come back to the manufacturer with a new order? Time will tell. But the sales manager has given this situation his best effort by a) delivering the bad news honestly, b) suggesting workable alternatives, and c) treating the customer with respect. One thing is for sure: a flat turndown—"No, you're not getting a thing from us beyond your warranty"—would have soured business relations permanently.

Although employees do not usually write claim memos to the company, they do send forward complaints in various forms. A manager's bad news response to a complaint about work conditions is on the next page. Notice in this response that the manager dignifies the complaint, not belittles it; conveys the bad news respectfully, not vindictively; and concludes with a statement of goodwill, not peevishness.

Sure, it's a small thing—one employee was too hot, and decided to write the big boss about it. But employer-employee relations are built up, for better or worse, by such small encounters. In this case, the manager took a few minutes to check into the situation and to say "no" to the employee's request for cooler temperatures. The bad news was delivered tactfully, however, with room left open for further discussion.

The manager could have chosen to belittle the complainer—"Bill, you're the only person who thinks the office is too hot"—or ridicule the complaint—"you seem to think I have nothing else to worry about besides the air conditioning thermostat!" Wisely, however, the manager listens to the complaint, makes a decision, and communicates it respectfully.

SUMMARY KEYS TO DELIVERING BAD NEWS MESSAGES

1. Use buffers to take the emotional edge off bad news that you know will disappoint or anger the message recipient.

2. Include an explanation for your "no" decision when circumstances allow. Do not feel obligated to justify each and every "no" decision.

3. Explanations given for "no" decisions should be truthful and nonmanipulative.

July 3, 199___

    To: William Tolson
          Marketing

  From: Ellen Rogers
          Director, Marketing and Sales

Subject: Your Concerns about Work Environment
          Temperatures

Bill, I understand from your lengthy memo of July 1 that you feel your work area is too warm during sunny afternoons. You requested any data I have on this matter and ask that I take action.

Here's my follow-up. The Climate Engineering office tells me that room temperatures in your area are between 78 and 80 degrees during even the warmest summer days. Under our agreement with the Environmental Protection Agency for energy savings, the company has committed not to turn down air conditioning below these temperature levels during the summer.

I hope you'll let me know immediately if room temperatures rise above the 80 degree limit. If you feel we need to work out some special arrangement for your continued work efficiency, please contact my secretary so we can find time to meet.

CHAPTER 6

HERE'S A MIXED BAG

*Good News
and Bad
News*

A mixed-bag message . . . should aim for one predominant effect upon the reader.

Many letters and memos in daily business include both good and bad news. You write to tell your sales people that their commission rates have been increased, but their territories decreased in size. You write to tell customers that their orders will be shipped, but not at your expense, as the customers had requested.

At such time, what goes where? Should good news always come before bad, or vice versa? Should you create a good news sandwich, with a slab of bad news in the middle? And how do you make smooth transitions between good news and bad? ("And now for something entirely different . . .")

These are the kinds of dilemmas that make mixed-bag messages some of the most poorly written (and, therefore, most dangerous) communications in business. In this chapter, we won't settle for blanket answers; the placement of good and bad news in a letter or memo depends upon your purpose, your reader, and the circumstances.

But we will emphasize one guiding principle: A mixed-bag message, though composed of contrasting parts, is one communication and should aim for one predominant effect upon the reader.

MIXED RESPONSES TO ORDERS, INQUIRIES AND REQUESTS

Put yourself in the shoes of a customer. You placed an urgent order, and now you receive a confirming letter. Would you prefer to read the good news first—that the company can fill the order—or the bad news—that it will arrive a few days after your big sale?

For the writer, the key here is not so much the arrangement of good and bad news as the connection between the two. Notice in this "before" and "after" version how the proper connection between good and bad news makes all the difference to the customer.

"Before" version:

Dear Mr. Herbert:

Thank you for your order #2983 received January 11, 199___. Be assured that it will be filled carefully and completely, and shipped to you via U.P.S. overnight service as you requested.

Because of assembly delays, we will not be able to fill the entire order until Feb. 1. We trust this delay does not inconvenience you.

We appreciate your business and look forward to serving you in the future.

After reading this letter, the customer wails, "Those idiots! I don't even want the order if it can't get here by January 25th for my sale. I told them to deliver by the 25th!" In the "after" revision, the proper connection between good news and bad news prevents such apoplexy on the customer's part, and probably saves the sale.

"After" revision:

Dear Mr. Herbert:

We're eager to fill your order #2983 received January 11, 199___. But first we want to make sure that our shipping schedule meets your needs.

Because of assembly delays, we will be able to ship 60 percent of your order to arrive by January 25, and the balance to arrive Feb. 1, both by U.P.S. overnight. Will 60 percent of the total order be sufficient for the sale period you describe in your letter?

Please contact us as soon as possible by FAX (389-2903) or phone (392-9939) regarding your wishes. We appreciate your order and want to fill it to your satisfaction.

In this "after" version, the customer recognizes from the beginning that the company understands the situation.

When responding to requests and invitations, you must be the judge (based on your purpose, audience, and circumstance) whether good news should precede or follow bad news in a mixed-bag message. Here are examples of each arrangement for both requests (memo form) and invitations (letter form).

May 11, 199__

    To: Lisa Reardon
           Product Development

  From: Barbara Walsh
           Vice President

Subject: Your Request for Additional Computing
           Resources

I have approved your request for six additional computing stations for Seventh Floor operations.

However, I think we can save money by purchasing six "dumb" terminals linked to a single file-server rather than acquiring six stand-alone PCs, as you requested. My approval, therefore, is contingent on your acceptance of this change.

I've passed along the purchase authorization to Lee Harvest (ext. 2983). Please contact him if you're ready to proceed, or give me a call if you have questions or concerns (ext. 8923).

Here is an alternate way of presenting the preceding message, with bad news first:

I think we can save money, Lisa, by purchasing "dumb" terminals linked to a single file-server rather than the six stand-alone PCs you request.

With this change, I have sent along an approved purchase authorization for the equipment to Lee Harvest (ext. 2983). Please contact him if you're ready to proceed, or give me a call if you have questions or concerns (ext. 8923).

Which version is best? The answer to that question depends upon your knowledge of Lisa Reardon, your reader. If Lisa will be pleased enough by your approval to swallow your rather high-handed change in her order, then put the good news first. But if you think Lisa prefers to tie up loose ends before moving ahead, present the bad news regarding your change before the good news of your approval.

Here are alternate versions of a mixed bag response to an invitation.

Dear Mr. Billings:

It will give me genuine pleasure to speak to your Rotary Club on Feb. 8 regarding my years as a research scientist for the Navy.

Unfortunately, I won't be able to speak, as you request, about developments in the SO4 atomic submarine program. Design and performance aspects of that project are classified.

I'm sure, however, that we can settle upon another topic of interest to your members. Please give me a call (392-3892) so that we can make arrangements.

With best regards,

Samuel R. Benton

Samuel R. Benton, Ph.D.

Notice in this letter the writer's confidence that the Rotary Club wants him for a speaker, whether or not he can talk on the requested topic. In an alternate version, the writer leaves open the possibility that the group may only want him to speak on the submarine project or not at all:

> *Thanks for your kind invitation to speak to the Rotary Club on Feb. 8. Unfortunately, the topic you suggest—SO4 submarine developments—is still classified.*
>
> *I am available to speak on this date, however, on other topics related to naval research. Please give me a call (392-3892) so we can discuss the interests of your group.*

MIXED BAG MESSAGES IN CREDIT COMMUNICATIONS

Letters and memos granting credit are usually made up not only of the good news—you've got credit—but also a laundry list of terms and conditions that, read closely, may constitute mild bad news.

As a general rule, place the good news of credit approval by itself at the beginning of the message. Give the reader at least this brief moment to bask in the satisfaction of being a potential debtor. Then, in the later paragraphs, spell out the various restrictions, limitations, and other contractual realities affecting the credit line.

Dear Ms. Owens:

Kendall Wholesale Supply is pleased to grant your request for a retailer's credit line in the amount of $25,000.

As described in the accompanying credit disclosure brochure, interest at a rate of 18 percent per annum will be charged on unpaid balances exceeding 30 days. No interest is charged if payment is received within 30 days.

Signators to the credit purchasing plan are limited to those listed on page 2 of your application form. The company reserves the right to approve any additional signators.

On behalf of our 286 employees, I'm happy to welcome you to the group of more than 3800 retailers now served by Kendall Wholesale Supply.

But if your credit-related message is predominantly negative, place the bad news first, after an appropriate buffer:

Dear Ms. Owens:

Thank you for contacting us regarding credit purchasing. At present, we are not able to open a credit line in the amount you request. (You can review your credit file without charge by calling Dunn & Bradstreet, 392-3892, within 60 days of receiving this letter.)

Many of our most established customers prefer to take advantage of the 5 percent cash discount offered by Kendall Wholesale Supply. The enclosed catalog describes both the discount program (p. 7) and our Spring line.

We hope to serve your needs in the near future.

MIXED BAG MESSAGES IN RESPONSES TO COMPLAINTS AND CLAIMS

Customer service representatives and others who do business with the public would have easier lives if messages sent to these audiences said simply, "yes, your claim is granted," or "no, get lost."

In the real world, however, many communications to customers and public stakeholders are mixed messages. The placement of good news and bad news depends on the now-familiar "big three": your purpose, your reader, and the circumstance.

If, for example, your goal is to clear up your reader's misunderstandings or educate him or her on proper procedures, you may choose to place your good news toward the end of the letter or memo. In this way, you hold the reader's attention. (After the good news, the reader may have little motive to read on.)

In the following memo, a manager makes clear to an employee that proper channels weren't used (the bad news) even though the employee's complaint will be resolved (the good news).

February 6, 199___

To: Morton Fairley
Accounting

From: Hanna Roth
Accounting Supervisor

Subject: Resolving Your Lighting Problems

I was surprised to hear from Bob Foster, our division manager, that you had written to him regarding flickering and buzzing light fixtures in your office. Mr. Foster has asked me to look into the matter.

As a matter of common practice, Morton, you should contact your work unit leader or me about such items. When a message goes forward directly to Mr. Foster, he can't help but assume that you've already tried (and failed) to get help from your immediate supervisors.

As for the problem itself, I've contacted Building Repair (as you could have—extension 982) and the problem will be resolved by Friday. Let me know if you have concerns about this or other aspects of your work environment.

And in the next letter, a customer service representative educates a customer about warranty terms before compromising (the good news) to make the problem go away.

Dear Mr. Williams:

I understand from the homeware department head (Linda King) at our Cambridge store that you returned an air conditioner to her department and asked for a complete refund. According to Ms. King, you presented a receipt showing that you bought the air conditioner from our store 18 months ago (July 7, 19___). She has referred the matter to me for resolution.

The warranty accompanying your air conditioner provides for one year parts and labor service. It is the policy of this company to offer a complete refund for a one-year period from date of purchase. Since you purchased your air conditioner 18 months ago, neither the warranty nor the refund policy any longer applies.

Nevertheless, we are eager to see you satisfied with your purchase. The manufacturer has authorized me to extend your warranty period for one additional month, during which time the air conditioner will be repaired without expense to you.

If this plan meets with your approval, please call Ms. King (982-3892) at your earliest convenience to arrange for repairs.

Sincerely,

Alice Roper

Alice Roper
Customer Service

SUMMARY KEYS IN WRITING MIXED-BAG MESSAGES

1. Decide where to place good news and bad news according to your purpose, your reader, and your circumstances.

2. Delay bad news if your reader won't read beyond it to the good news.

3. Delay good news if your reader won't read beyond it to neutral information or necessary bad news.

CHAPTER 7

THE EXTENDED LETTER

Reports and Proposals

Letter or memo reports and proposals are usually less than five pages long.

L et's say that you face a choice: you can read a ten-page report or two-page condensation of the same report in memo form. Which would you choose?

If your in-basket resembles a paper blizzard, you'll probably opt for the shorter form. In the 1990s, so do most managers across industries. Like you, these men and women face more and more words to read each day, thanks to modern "time-savers" such as word-processing, high-speed printing, high-tech photocopying, and electronic mail. When it comes to business documents, most professionals would agree "the shorter the better."

This chapter discusses how to use letter and memo formats to write brief reports and proposals. In doing so, the writer maintains two features of the conventional letter or memo:

- the layout (block, modified block, or simplified for letters, or memo format)
- the conversational style, particularly in the first paragraph of the letter or memo

In addition, three features are borrowed from traditional reports and proposals:

- headings (and, for longer documents, subheadings)
- graphs, charts, and tables as required
- in-text complete citation of sources. (Letter or memo reports and proposals rarely include a section of Works Cited, endnotes, or footnotes.)

Letter or memo reports and proposals are usually less than five pages long.

THE USES OF THE LETTER AND MEMO REPORTS

The letter form is used to report out-of-company audiences, including clients, regulators, community representatives, shareholders, and others. The memo form is used to report to in-house audiences, including various levels of management and other departments.

The letter and memo report is commonly used for:

- problem assessments and analyses
- trip reporting
- laboratory and test recording
- procedural and policy reports
- feasibility studies
- progress reporting
- periodic reporting

THE LOGIC OF THE LETTER AND MEMO REPORT

No matter what the use, most letter and memo reports follow a similar developmental pattern:

Opening (first paragraph) Conversational statement of purpose for the ensuing material.

Topic or Problem Statement (second paragraph) Specific description of the topic or problem under discussion.

Necessary Background (third paragraph, or combined with second paragraph) A concise history of the topic or problem. No more background is given than is necessary for the reader to understand the material at hand.

Significant Developments (middle paragraphs, as required) Description and/or analysis of current action or thinking with regard to the topic or problem.

Assessment (middle paragraphs, as required) An evaluation of what is working and what remains to be done.

Conclusion, with *Recommendations* (final paragraphs) Summary statement of results, with specific recommendations for future action. (Note that the Conclusions and Recommendations section may also be placed at the beginning of the letter or memo report, following the Opening. In that case, the letter or memo report would conclude with a brief summary statement.)

Appropriate Well-wishing, Appreciation, and *Contact Information* (last sentences) Final thanks, if appropriate, to the reader and information on where questions and comments can be directed.

THE LETTER REPORT

Each of the categories above usually forms a section of the letter report set off by a heading (as illustrated in the following sample). Note that the headings are content-specific (that is, they include words that refer to the content of the report) and that Roman numerals are not used for headings. A subject line is often used to take the place of the title that would appear in traditional report formatting.

A Sample Letter Report

June 8, 199__

Ms. Helen Kent, Vice President
SuperBuy Grocery Markets, Inc.
92 Lester Road
Boston, MA 01829

SUBJECT: Presentations at the Annual Managers Meeting

Dear Ms. Kent:

It was good to see you again at the National Food Industry Council meeting, and I was glad to hear about your recent promotion at SuperBuy. Congratulations! As you requested, I'm writing to offer ideas for making your annual meetings more effective.

Since our discussion, I have read participant evaluations from the last four SuperBuy managers meetings and have spoken with many managers and senior executives in your company. In general, these sources judge the annual meetings to be an unproductive use of time—"boring," "repetitive," "just a lot of talking," and "amateurish" are recurring descriptions. My report assesses the information provided by these sources and offers recommendations for more effective annual meetings.

A Brief History of the Annual Managers Meeting

SuperBuy began holding annual managers meetings in 1975. The first five meetings (1975–1979) were organized and run by a professional meeting planner, who brought in several "name" presenters. Attendees simply sat back and watched the show.

As costs for such services rose, however, SuperBuy's CEO (Eric Wetherspoon) decided to use in-house talent in place of paid presenters. Through 1985, Wetherspoon and other top executives themselves made the major presentations at the annual meeting. This practice ended abruptly after a 1985 survey showed that 85 percent of managers attending the meeting found these executive briefings to be uninspiring, redundant, and poorly prepared.

For the 1986 meeting, the company's new CEO (Sheila Morgan) selected rank-and-file managers as speakers for the meeting. Over a period of two days, a total of ten one-hour speeches was delivered by ten managers at that meeting. Response from participants was highly favorable. Although the presentations were far from professional, they dealt with down-to-earth issues in terms that managers understood. This format for meeting speakers has continued to the present.

Current Controversy and Complaints Among Speakers

A few days after the 1991 annual managers meeting, the CEO received a letter of complaint signed by all ten managers/speakers for that meeting. The letter pointed out that "we are not trained professional speakers, and therefore should not be asked to make presentations before large audiences unless we also receive adequate training to do so. For many of us, the process of developing a presentation and delivering it was a professional nightmare that included serious bouts with speaker's nerves, dozens of uncompensated hours of preparation in addition to our usual duties, and little assistance from the company in the preparation of necessary slides and other visual aids."

Based on this letter and subsequent meetings with these speakers, the CEO has decided to make as-yet undefined changes in how speakers are selected for next year's meeting.

**Evaluation of Speakers' and
Participants' Responses**

All parties to the annual meeting (including the CEO, top management, the speakers, and participating managers) seem to agree on two points:

1. In-house speakers are preferable to out-of-house speakers.
2. Managers are preferable as speakers to top management.

In addition, most meeting attendees have been favorably impressed by the managers' speeches, even though the speakers themselves felt their efforts to be somewhat amateurish.

The key point, however, is the stress described by managers who are selected to give speeches. Many have been so terrified by the idea of speaking before an audience of 1000 or more that they sought out professional counseling and medical aid to get them through the experience. Others say that they have considered quitting their jobs because of the burden of speech preparation and delivery.

The solution to these problems, according to the presenting managers, lies in adequate speech coaching and company assistance in preparing visual aids.

Conclusion, with Recommendations

In summary, the company is at an impasse: the CEO wants managers to speak, but they resist doing so without support from the company in the form of speech coaching and assistance in producing visual aids.

Since the company saves more than $50,000 each meeting by not employing outside professional speakers, a small portion of those funds (perhaps $5,000 to $10,000) should be devoted to expert speech coaching for the selected managers. An additional amount (perhaps $3,000–$4,000) can be spent on the production of professional visual aids.

Recommendations:

1. Interview and retain a speech consultant to work closely with selected managers in the preparation of their material and development of their delivery skills.
2. Determine whether in-house audiovisual services can provide support in the production of visual aids for speakers. If not, an outside firm should be retained for this purpose.
3. Survey the responses of speakers and attendees at this year's meeting to assess the effectiveness of speech coaching and visual aid assistance.

I recognize, Helen, that this matter has fallen in your lap as one of your new job responsibilities. Don't hesitate to call me to discuss any of these ideas. I would also be glad to suggest a list of reputable speech consultants in your area.

Good luck with your planning for this year's meeting, and best personal regards.

Cordially,

Robert R. Henderson

Robert R. Henderson
Director
Food Industry Institute

If Henderson worked within the SuperBuy organization, this same information could have been cast in the form of a memo report, using the typical To: From: Subject: headings.

THE MEMO REPORT

In the following example, the memo format has been used for a trip report. Note that the elements of topic statement, background, developments, assessment, and conclusion/recommendations are still present, although named in content-specific language in the headings.

April 14, 199__

To: Roger Wilson
    Manager

From: Forest Thompson
      Sales Associate

Subject: Results of Business Trip to Miami area, April
         4–9, 199__.

We already discussed by phone some of the results of my Miami trip, Roger, but I want to sum up matters in a complete way by this memo.

Assigned Travel

From April 4–9, I visited four companies in the greater Miami area: Likert Mills, Brenton Carpets, Western Fabric Supply, and Anderson Home Systems. Each of these firms wholesales more than $15 million of residential and commercial carpeting each year. The purpose of my sales call was to assess their use of stain-blocking treatments and to promote our new product, STAINGUARD.

Background

Until 1988, none of these companies pretreated its carpeting with a stain-blocker. Two of the companies (Brenton and Anderson) sold an after-installation spot remover comparable to commercially available sprays such as Spot-Out and Sani-Clean.

With the growing use of stain-blocking nylon fibres beginning in 1988, all four companies began searching for ways to pretreat all their carpets, including nylons and nylon blends, with some cost-effective stain-blocker. Market research (Livingston, 1989; Torvald, 1990) demonstrated the attractiveness of the "stain-blocker" concept for retail purchasers.

Likert and Western developed their own in-house treatments, while Brenton and Anderson experimented with a chemical treatment originally intended for odor removal. To date, none of the companies reports satisfaction with their chosen processes.

Nature of Sales Calls

At extended meetings with company decision-makers at each firm, I demonstrated the STAINGUARD product and pointed out independent laboratory evaluations of its effectiveness. Using samples of their own carpeting, I showed the efficacy of STAINGUARD treatment to prevent staining by wine, sodas, fruit juices, food residues and common inks.

Following this demonstration, I explained how STAINGUARD can be applied as an easy step in the carpet manufacturing process. Together with their accounting personnel, I calculated approximate costs per yard for the STAINGUARD difference.

Assessment of Customer Responses

My demonstrations were received very favorably at all four companies. Executives at Brenton and Western seemed especially impressed by the cost savings accrued through the use of STAINGUARD when compared to their present stain-prevention treatment. Management at Likert and Anderson requested phone numbers of companies now using STAINGUARD, and I provided these references.

Conclusion, with Recommendations

I felt that the Miami trip was worthwhile in promoting STAINGUARD to four well-known carpet manufacturers. Use of our product by any one of them would attract significant interest by other carpet manufacturers throughout the area.

To lead these four companies from interest to actual purchase, our technical staff must be prepared to give them specific guidance on how the STAINGUARD step can best be integrated into their present manufacturing process.

Recommendations:

1. Authorize our technical staff to prepare preliminary installation descriptions of STAINGUARD equipment for each manufacturer.
2. Authorize return travel to the Miami area in mid-May for me and a technical representative. On this trip we will present installation suggestions and, I'm confident, bring back significant orders.

If you have questions or comments, Roger, give me a call (ext. 198). I'll be in the office all this week.

LETTER AND MEMO PROPOSALS

Proposals are similar to reports in that they both begin by addressing a particular problem or topic, giving background information, and evaluating current developments. The proposal differs from the report, however, in providing specific details about a plan of action to achieve particular goals. For example, a report on inadequate electrical service to a plant might focus on the problem and recommend that money be budgetted to repair the problem. A proposal on the same topic would also focus on the problem, but would go on to propose a specific plan (including information about equipment, personnel, facilities, and expenditures) to resolve the problem.

Letter and memo proposals are often written by contractors. If the proposal is accepted, a formal contract authorizing work will be signed.

The Letter Proposal

In the following letter proposal, an office design firm proposes to remodel an office on the accounting floor of a major corporation. The purpose of this proposal is to obtain authorization in concept for work proposed. Specific renderings of space usage and proposed furnishings will be provided by the contractor after the initial proposal has been accepted. (In this way, contractors avoid "spinning their wheels"—performing expensive planning work on behalf of companies who haven't yet decided to become clients.)

March 19, 199___

Mr. Ted Ainsworth
Managing Partner
Western Cities Architectural Design, Inc.
892 Star Drive
San Francisco, CA 98232

SUBJECT: Proposal for Redesign of Accounting Wing

Dear Mr. Ainsworth:

I want to thank you and your executive committee for meeting with Lisa Johnson and me last Thursday. We are delighted that you like our preliminary suggestions for cost-effective remodeling of your accounting facilities.

In this letter, I want to sum up our discussions so far and propose the next steps in seeing this project on its way to reality.

Project Background

During the past decade, almost every sector of your Star Drive headquarters has been remodeled for the efficient and attractive use of space. Only the accounting area (6th floor) still maintains its 1950ish bureaucratic look: desks in straight rows without separating partitions, outmoded lighting, unattractive wall coverings and decor, and brown vinyl flooring.

Due in large part to such unattractive work surroundings, your company has had trouble attracting and retaining qualified accounting personnel. Data from hiring interviews and exit interviews confirm the consensus among accounting personnel that their work area, in the words of a former accounting employee, "looks like and feels like a mental morgue."

Current Project Status

The accounting department traditionally experiences a slow period in their work requirements in the weeks following tax season (ending April 15). During these works, it will be possible to move accounting personnel to temporary quarters on the fourth floor.

Assuming that the proposed remodeling can be completed within 30 days from initiation shortly after April 15, the accounting department can be up and running again on the sixth floor by mid-May.

Proposed Specifics

Office Design, Inc., proposes a modular reorganization of the sixth floor office space, as depicted in Elevation A (attached). In this design, each accountant would work within his or her own space defined by partitions and planted areas. Wide corridors between such spaces will maintain the open feel of the area as well as easy physical access to work spaces.

State-of-the-art furniture (see attached List of Recommended Furniture) has been chosen to compliment a harmonious room design while at the same time supporting the work needs of accountants. The model #792 desk, for example, makes special provision for a desktop PC, drawers for hard copy spread sheets, and security drawers for proprietary and sensitive documents.

Remodeling will be undertaken in five stages:

> *Stage One* April 18–23 Removal of existing furnishings, wall- and floor-coverings.
> *Stage Two* April 24–30 Surface preparation of walls and floors for new coverings.
> *Stage Three* May 1–5 Installation of diaphragm lighting system.
> *Stage Four* May 6–10 Installation of new wall- and floor-coverings.

Stage Five May 11–14 Installation of office furniture and plants.

Western Cities Architectural Design will not be required to supply any personnel, including janitorial staff, for purposes of this work. All workers performing labor for Office Design, Inc., will be bonded and insured. It will be the responsibility of Office Design, Inc., to obtain all necessary permits and inspections for the proposed work.

Schedule of Fees

Payment for the proposed work is requested in three installments:

1. $45,000 retainer upon acceptance of this proposal
2. $50,000 at the completion of Stage Three
3. $50,000 at the completion of Stage Five and project sign-off by City inspectors.

Total consideration: $145,000.

Conclusion

We invite your close attention to the renderings and furniture brochures accompanying this proposal. As you review these materials, please feel free to call upon us with any questions or concerns. If you approve this project proposal, our legal counsel can meet with yours to draw up mutually acceptable contracts reflecting the terms described above.

Thank you for considering the services of Office Design, Inc. We look forward to working with you.

Sincerely,

Ellen O. Wilson
Vice President

The Memo Proposal

Good ideas spawned within a business organization often die because no one takes the time to commit them to paper in the form of a memo proposal. No matter how appealing the idea, it usually cannot be passed along to higher levels of review and approval in verbal form. Someone has to write it down.

In the following memo proposal, a mid-level manager describes a better way to control absenteeism. Many companies award bonuses for employee ideas that lead to better work efficiency or morale.

January 11, 199___

To: Patricia R. Roberts
Operations Vice President

From: James Long
Manager, Division 6

Subject: A Plan for Significant Reductions in Employee
Absenteeism

In your general memo of Dec. 10, you invite company employees to write up ideas that may save the company money and improve the work environment. I appreciate your consideration of my proposal for a sick family member facility here at our headquarters to reduce employee absenteeism.

Background of the Absenteeism Problem

In my division, a total of 212 employees took 1,418 sick days during the last fiscal year. The expense to the company in lost labor was approximately $260,500. If that same ratio is true for the company's 750 other employees, then the company is losing more than $1 million per year to sick days.

I conducted a survey of these employees to determine, on an anonymous basis, whether their sick time was in fact being used because of their own illness or because of that of family members, including children and elderly parents.

Of the 160 survey forms returned, 46 percent of the employees said that at least half their sick days were taken not for themselves but for family members in their care. In the vast majority of these cases, the illnesses involved were neither serious nor long-lasting: colds, flu, stomach upsets, and so forth.

Company Options

As the number of elderly increases in our society and the number of children per family begins to rise again (after a 20-year decline), we can expect our employees to be taking even more sick time for the care of these family members.

Or the company can act in its own interest and that of its employees to establish a sick family-member room coordinated with the company infirmary. Cost savings, as calculated below, would amount to at least $150,000 per year, with the additional advantage of improved employee morale and significant recruitment advantages.

Proposal Specifics

1. At present, Room D at the company health center is not used. I propose that it be furnished with four hospital beds and appropriate furnishings. Approximate cost: $5,000.
2. Two health officers (Dr. White and Nurse Evans) now maintain services at the company. I propose that a licensed practical nurse (LPN) be hired to assist them in the additional care required for Room D patients. Approximate cost: $35,000 per year.
3. Finally, I propose that the Executive Committee work together with Dr. White and Nurse Evans to define standards for admittance to the health center.

If the availability of a sick family-member room were pub-
licized to employees, the company stands to save hundreds
of thousands of dollars. Precise calculations can be made at
such times as final costs are determined for set-up of the
facility and employee use patterns become apparent.

Conclusion

I urge you to consider this low-cost and practical plan to
reduce absenteeism. If I can be helpful in further employee
surveys or other aspects of this project, please feel free to
call on me.

LETTER AND MEMO REPORTS AND PROPOSALS IN THE FAX AGE

The burgeoning use of FAX and electronic mail in the
officeplace makes letter and memo reports and proposals
all the more attractive. Although we may thumb through
a 15-page traditional report that lands on our desk in sta-
pled form, we may not receive it so kindly as it curls like
a long, long snake out of our FAX machine. We may be
even less inclined to read such a lengthy document on-
screen through e-mail.

The letter or memo format for reports and proposals,
in short, shows every sign of becoming even more popular
as the Electronic Revolution sweeps through business,
industry, and government. The ability to write such documents with skill is a "must have" for upwardly mobile
professionals.

CHAPTER 8

CHANGING AND REARRANGING

Fast Fixes for the Final Polish

The final "look" of your document matters as much as all the hard work you've poured into its language and content.

Count on it: the last five minutes you spend on your letter or memo are infinitely more valuable than the first five minutes you spend on it.

Unfortunately, many business writers skip that last five minutes. You know the result. Letters and memos go out filled with errors in fact, logic, spelling, grammar, and punctuation. Just as serious are unrevised errors in tone— those snarling or petty messages that, with a moment's review, would have been (and should have been) reconsidered.

LEARNING TO LIKE REVISION

Like revision? That's a tall order, especially when business writing itself may not be high on your list of cuddly things.

Writers sometimes have the mistaken notion that revision is a form of assassination—killing inch by inch the gorgeous flow of the first draft. They associate revision with a Mr. or Ms. Gradgrind, English instructor, at some time in their education. Picky, picky, picky.

But contrast that negative mindset with the attitudes of other creators toward their works. A painter looks at the final touchups of a painting as perfecting it, not fretting it. A musician looks forward to checking out the notes for the final score; without such checking, the performance may sound lke fingernails on a blackboard. Writers, too, should learn to revise with pleasure.

A STEP-BY-STEP PLAN FOR REVISION

The final check-out and revision of letters and memos may be more palatable if it happens in five quick steps.

Step One Does your main message stand out?

Reread your letter or memo from the point of view of your reader. Can you quickly locate the clear, concise statement of your main message? Or is it found here and there all over the page, half-buried in long paragraphs?

Solutions:

- Use short, direct sentences to state your main message.
- Put your main message in a short paragraph by itself.
- Tell your reader when you reach your main idea: "Here's what I conclude . . . I can sum up the situation as follows . . . The most important point is . . ."

Step Two Will your language appeal to your reader?

Think about the words you've used in your letter or memo. How will your reader interpret those words? Will your message sound too bureaucratic? Too academic? Too slangy or chatty?

Solutions:

- Trust common, simple words to carry your meaning. Use jargon and "intellectual" verbiage only when such words communicate better than any others.
- Read your message aloud. Wherever your language sounds awkward or obtuse, use your ordinary conversational phrasing of the idea as your best guide.

Step Three Do your ideas hang together logically and persuasively?

Readers don't like to reassemble your thoughts like a jigsaw puzzle to determine your intended message. Think through the progress of your ideas to make sure they link up in a clear, cogent way.

Solutions:

- As you reread your message, mentally paraphrase the gist of your idea in each paragraph. You'll quickly discover whether your ideas march in a straight line.
- Review the *Ten Most Common Logical Errors* appended to this chapter. Reread your message with a sharp eye out for their presence.

Step Four Is your letter or memo free of surface errors?

How would you feel taking advice from a financial counselor who couldn't add? Going to a physician who misspells the name of the operation you'll undergo? In the same way, your credibility depends in part upon your mastery of all the little things in writing—correct spelling, grammar, usage, punctuation, capitalization, and so forth. The "Basic (Ugh) Grammar" guide at the end of this book covers most of the items that matter most (and are missed most by business writers).

Solutions:

- Use a spell-checker (such as *SpellStar* or *CorrectStar*), but don't depend on it to correct incorrect word forms ("bare" where you intended "bear," "it" where you intended "is.")
- Read your document aloud to discover omitted words. The eye skips quickly past portions of the sentence that the voice won't ignore.
- Scan your letter or memo from back to front to pick up spelling mistakes. Reading forward makes us aware of content more than word forms; reading backward highlights the words themselves.

Step Five How does your letter or memo look on the page?

The final "look" of your document matters as much as all the hard work you've poured into its language and content. Examine your paragraphs: Too many long ones? Too many short ones? Check out your margins: Wide enough for easy reading? Consistent from page to page? Look over your lists and inset passages: Have bullets or numbers been used correctly? Are items within lists worded in parallel structure for easy comparison? Consider your fonts and printing medium: Does the message look dark, crisp and clear on the page? Have you used italics, boldface, and graphic highlights appropriately? Check for letter or memo elements: Have you included all the components you wished, including reference initials, copy notations, and enclosures?

Solutions:

- Ask a co-worker or friend to look over your final draft and make suggestions for its improvement. (You don't always have to make such changes, but at least you've had the advantage of another person's point of view.)
- Set the document aside for a few hours, then review it at your leisure. In the heat of composition, what looks "good enough" may cry out for revision a few hours later.
- Look at memos or letters you've received from the people you're writing to. Do you spot any aspect of their style or format that you should imitate in your messaging? For example, if they have signed their letters "Cordially," should yours end with "Sincerely"? [Probably not.] If they type their name to include "Dr.," should you address your letter to "Ms." or "Mr."? [Again, probably not.]

TEN COMMON PITFALLS IN LETTER AND MEMO LOGIC

1. Circular Reasoning. What was supposed to be an explanation turns out to be a mere restatement.

All employees are encouraged to participate in after-hours company recreation programs because such programs are especially for the use of employees after the workday has ended.

2. Hasty Generalization. The conclusion reached is based on too little evidence.

Democrats can't win the election because of their stand on animal rights.

3. Non Sequitur. A conclusion is reached that does not follow from the evidence presented.

Johnson owns two homes, a boat, and a sports car. I trust his investment advice.

4. Bias. Personal opinions and viewpoints become the standard for evaluating objective arguments.

Ms. Wilmington has every right to apply for the new position. But she won't get it. I just don't want to work with a woman.

5. Either/Or Thinking. Two alternatives are presented as the only alternatives.

Either he apologizes or I quit.

6. False Cause. An earlier occurrence is incorrectly presented as the cause of a later event.

We switched to leased cars instead of company-owned cars in 1984. No wonder we have so many auto repair bills each month!

7. Straw Man. A false target is set up for the main thrust of an argument. Knocking over the straw man creates the illusion that the argument has succeeded.

This company's problems can be blamed on poor benefits. How can anyone expect workers to concentrate on their jobs when they have doubts about their medical and dental coverage?

8. Faulty Syllogism. A pattern of thought leads to an unjustifiable conclusion.

All managers wear moustaches. I wear a moustache. Therefore, I must be a manager.

9. Stacking the Argument. Presenting evidence on behalf of one side of the argument while ignoring evidence on the other side.
Undersea mining operations are dangerous, expensive, time-consuming, and unreliable. We should not consider undersea mining in deciding how and where to mine for gold.

10. False Elimination. From an array of possible alternatives, one by one is eliminated until only one alternative remains. The illusion is thereby created that the final alternative is the best.
In reviewing cities for our company move, we've seen why Toledo, Miami, Dallas, Chicago, and Milwaukee won't meet our needs. That leaves Phoenix as our new company home.

COMMON MISSPELLED WORDS IN BUSINESS

absence	attendance	disappearance
accidentally	beginning	disastrous
accommodate	beneficial	dissatisfied
accumulate	benefited	effect
advice	break	eligible
advise	Britain	embarrass
a lot	bureau	eminent
allot	business	environment
amateur	choose	equipped
analyze	chose	especially
appearance	committee	exaggerate
arctic	conscience	excellence
arguing	conscious	existence
argument	definitely	experience
arithmetic	desperate	familiar
athletic	dictionary	February

Reprinted with permission, Arthur H. Bell, *Business Communication: Toward 2000* Cincinnati: South-Western Publishing, 1991.

COMMON MISSPELLED WORDS IN BUSINESS

foreign
forty
fourth
generally
government
grammar
height
heiress
homemade
humorous
hygiene
immediately
incredible
independence
interesting
irresistible
its, it's
laid
lead
led
lightning
loneliness
loose
lose
losing
marriage
mathematics
maybe
miniature
miracle
mysterious
necessary
neurotic
ninety
notable
noticeable
occurred

occurrence
omitted
optimistic
parallel
paralyze
pastime
performance
personal
personnel
physical
possession
precede
preferred
prejudice
principal
principle
privilege
probably
proceed
professor
pronunciation
prophecy
prophesy
qualm
quarrel
quiet
quite
quizzes
receive
receiving
referee
reference
referred
restaurant
rhythm
sacrilegious
schedule

seize
separate
sergeant
severely
sieve
similar
sophomore
stationary
stationery
studying
subtle
successful
surprise
tendency
than
then
their, there, they're
thorough
through
to, too, two
tragedy
tries
trouble
truly
typically
usually
unbelievable
utterance
vaccinate
vain
vein
villain
weather
weird
wholly
writing

CHAPTER 9

DIFFICULT LETTERS AND MEMOS

*Writing for
Sensitive
Situations*

What do you say when you disagree with the boss?

At his retirement party, one IBM executive recently quipped that he spent 80 percent of his writing time on only 5 percent of his letters and memos. He had in mind these five communications infamous for causing Writer's Block:

- discipline messages
- requests for raises or promotion
- apologies
- cover letters to accompany your resume
- objections

In these messages more than others, "tone is all"— how you say it matters at least as much as what you say.

PREPARING TO WRITE DIFFICULT MESSAGES

Begin by talking out your message as if your reader were physically present. If you get stuck, start again from the beginning until you can have your say, start to finish.

Do not set pen to paper or fingers to keys until you have not only a clear grasp of what you want to say but also the tone you want to maintain. One way to capture the tone you want is to jot down particularly appropriate phrases from your earlier "out loud" version of the message.

In the letters and memos that follow, we have tried to use generally appropriate language and tone. Your individual circumstances may require quite different words. We hope, however, that these samples suggest useful approaches to the difficult messages that, as one writer says, "cause drops of blood to pop out on the forehead."

The Discipline Message

There's no trick to writing a discipline message to someone headed out the door of the company. If you choose, you can unload both barrels on the misdoer and not lose a wink of sleep.

But a discipline message to an employee you want to or have to keep? That's a different matter. You have to find disciplinary language that leaves room for good working relations and incentives to improve. In short, you have to slap the hand you're holding.

In the following discipline memo, notice that the language focuses on behaviors (what the employee did) instead of on personal characteristic (what the employee is). This distinction leaves room for improvement. Most of us can change what we do, but not what we are.

In reading these messages, you will recognize that many of the situations they discuss would have been dealt with in a personal meeting as well as in writing.

January 8, 199__

 To: Lester Todd
     Security Specialist I

From: Martha Owens
      Staff Coordinator

Subject: Personal Goal-setting for Reduced Absenteeism

As we discussed yesterday in my office, Lester, your pattern of absenteeism poses a major problem to your continued employment. In the past three months, you have used five sick days without filing the required medical verification and have, in addition, been absent from work six times for the various "personal" reasons you explained to your supervisor.

I'm putting this reprimand in writing to you to underline the seriousness of your absenteeism.

I will consider the coming quarter a probationary period for you. Your supervisor will report to me on a weekly basis regarding your job attendance and performance. If you have unauthorized absences during this period, you will be dismissed. But with commitment on your part, I hope that we can put this matter behind us.

The company pays for extensive counseling services and other resources for employess. You must be the judge of whether these services can be of use to you in avoiding further absences. Jill Davis, Director of Counseling, will be happy to meet with you to describe the services of her center. You can call her at extension 898 to make an appointment.

On a personal level, Lester, I have seen the good work you're capable of and I want to do whatever I can to help you meet the job expectations of the company.

The Request for a Raise or Promotion

How do you blow your own horn without driving people away? In the following memo, a mid-level manager uses appreciation as the bridge to the more touchy matter of asking for a substantial raise. Notice that the manager doesn't threaten resignation in an explicit way or make claims about how much the competition will pay her. The memo concludes in such a way that the executive reader has some flexibility to respond. The memo would certainly be less successful if the reader had to make a rigid either/or decision.

September 8, 199___

   To: Linda Flower
        Vice President, Personnel

 From: Ruth Williams
        Personnel Specialist I

Subject: Your perspective on my career path

I've enjoyed my professional associations and work assignments over the past two years at XyTech. I feel a strong commitment to the company and its future.

I'm writing to ask you to consider me for the present opening in our department for Personnel Analyst. The published advertisement for this position specifies five years of prerequisite personnel experience. Although I haven't worked in the field that long, I'm confident I could perform well in this position for three reasons:

- I have just completed my M.A. in Human Resource Management at State University. My studies have given me a thorough knowledge of the latest theories and practical applications in HR and personnel responsibilities.

- I worked closely with Mark Atrim, the recently retired Personnel Analyst whose position is being filled. Mark asked me to assist him for a period of six months with the "Hire the Best" program. With his help, I learned a great deal about his job activities during that time.
- I have excellent working relations not only with coworkers in my department but with employees throughout the company. These relationships could prove invaluable to the work of the Personnel Analyst.

I would be happy to meet with you to discuss other aspects of my qualifications and preparation for this position. Thank you for your support over the past two years and for your consideration of my strong interest in the Personnel Analyst position.

Apologies

Whether in a letter to a client or a memo to a work associate, apologies are difficult to put into writing. You must say enough to communicate your sincerity, yet not so much as to seem self-punishing.

Here are the circumstances behind the following apology. An advertising account executive completely forgot about inviting a client to a business lunch. The client found himself waiting alone for an hour at a restaurant far from his office. For the account executive, there was no death in the family or car problem. He just blew it.

The following letter reinforces his earlier phone call of apology. Because the client contacted the account executive's boss to find out what happened, the account executive will probably file a blind copy of this apology letter with his boss to show that he has followed up.

April 19, 199___

John R. Robbins
Advertising Director
Tri-Cities Furniture, Inc.
98 Appletree Highway
Seattle, WA 98233

Dear John:

I'm writing to follow up on our phone conversation this morning. I want to repeat my apology for missing our lunch meeting on Monday. I really can't explain what happened; the meeting was very important to me, but I neglected to note it in my calendar. For some reason, I had in mind that we were meeting on Tuesday. At any rate, I feel terrible about my mistake.

I'd like to reschedule our meeting at your convenience — and this time at Chez Albert. I'll call you tomorrow to see if you're available. I do hope you'll give me this second chance. Believe me, your account executive will get to the restaurant early this time!

Thanks for your understanding.

With best regards,

Paul

Paul Neill
Account Executive

Cover Letter to Accompany Your Resume

What's left to say in a cover letter? Your resume has provided details about your education, experience, career goals, special skills, and references. Should a cover letter try to repeat this information in paragraphs?

No. A cover letter that repeats the resume ends up much too long for the applicant's good. In addition, a redundant cover letter can steal the thunder of the resume.

In recent surveys of Fortune 500 companies, personnel directors say that they give most of their attention to the resume, not the cover letter. In some cases, personnel directors said they gave only 20 to 30 seconds to a perusal of the cover letter.

In that short window of opportunity, a job applicant should try to accomplish four things:

- Name the job you want. Major companies may be advertising for dozens of different jobs on a given day. The cover letter must specify a particular job so that the application can be routed correctly within the company.
- Tell briefly where you heard about the job. If you're responding to an advertisement, tell where it appeared. If a company employee or mutual acquaintance told you about the opening, mention his or her name (with permission).
- Highlight one or two aspects of your resume that would be particularly interesting or impressive to the company. Don't try to repeat your resume. Your goal in the cover letter is to emphasize aspects of the resume so that they will stand out when the resume is read.
- Ask for an interview. You can increase your chances of obtaining an interview by sounding enthusiastic and indicating your flexibility as to interview time and place.

In the following cover letter, the job applicant has seen an ad in the *Washington Post*. She mentions the name of the newspaper, the date, and the advertisement number (not all ads have numbers) to aid the company in routing her application correctly.

June 19, 199__

Herbert R. Signum
Director of Personnel
General Manufacturing, Inc.
983 Seventh St.
Washington, DC 20883

Dear Mr. Signum:

I'm eager to be considered for the Public Relations staff position advertised in the Washington Post, June 18, advertisement #292.

As my attached resume suggests, I have worked in positions of progressive responsibility in the public relations area since receiving my B.A. in Marketing from Georgetown University. You may be particularly interested in my leadership role in two high-profile PR projects at Apple Computer: the "Take a Byte" campaign and the "Easy as Pie" program for school sales.

I'll be happy to meet with you at your convenience to learn more about your goals for public relations at General Manufacturing and to introduce myself more thoroughly. Feel free to call me at my office (202-389-2893) or at home (391-389-4893). Thank you for considering my strong desire to interview for this position.

Sincerely,

Nancy R. Jenson

Nancy R. Jenson
Public Relations Specialist

Objections

What do you say (or keep from saying) when you disagree with the boss? For lack of an answer to that question, many managers bite their tongues and simply stew. Better by far for the blood pressure and the corporation to explain your objection in a clear, respectful memo or letter.

In the following memo, a manager writes the most difficult objection of all—a challenge to the boss on a matter of ethics. The writer's goal is to stimulate the boss's thinking without awakening his ire. But above all, the writer wants to take a stand for the sake of her own conscience and ultimately, for the welfare of the company.

July 16, 199__

   To: Sean Thomas
       Director of Personnel

 From: Alice Trent
       Financial Analyst

Subject: Reconsideration of Recruitment Language

Sean, I'm concerned about a matter that involves both of our areas of responsibility. I'd like to "talk it out" in this memo, partly to ask your perspective on the subject and partly to firm up my own thinking.

As you know, we're under pressure as a company to show at least 50 employees with M.S. degrees on staff by August 1. Without them, we cannot qualify for federal contract #17A6, which requires this level of staff expertise when the federal contract is awarded.

Motivated by this pressure, your group has undertaken an aggressive recruitment campaign in the Silicon Valley region of California. Applications have begun to arrive from many California managers holding M.S. degrees.

At the same time, we're both aware from the CEO's internal document #8091 that layoffs of approximately 10 percent of the work force will begin on September 15 of this year.

The dilemma as I see it, Sean, is that we are knowingly recruiting men and women who will sell their homes and move their families across country to take positions with our company—positions that will evaporate as soon as we have qualified for minimum M.S. staffing levels for the federal contract.

No matter what the pressures upon us, I believe our present course is both manipulative and ethically indefensible. The most obvious losers in this situation will be the many employees who move across country for what turns out to be no more than 45 days of work. But the company stands to lose as well, I think, when this situation appears in the press (as it will) and is reviewed by federal contract regulators.

So for all these reasons—human, ethical, and practical—I urge you to reconsider the current recruitment strategy. I don't have a solution to this dilemma, Sean, but I see a train wreck ahead on the company's present track. I would value your opinion on the matter.

THE KEY TO DIFFICULT COMMUNICATIONS

Doing two or more dances at once leads inevitably to stumbling. In the same way, trying to be all things to all people in problematic business communications leads to Writer's Block or awkward expression.

Difficult communication becomes easier when the writer

- takes a stand
- communicates that position in a tactful but straightforward way
- conveys respect for the reader's motives and abilities.

Finally, trust a friend to read your draft of a difficult communication before you send it.

APPENDIX

RECOMMENDED REFERENCES

Consult these standard handbooks for more general and complete guidance:

Achtert, Walter S. and Joseph Gibaldi. *The MLA Style Manual.* New York: Modern Language Association, 1985.

American Psychological Association. *Publication Manual of the American Psychological Association,* third edition. Washington, DC: American Psychological Association, 1983.

(The) Chicago Manual of Style, fourteenth edition. Chicago: University of Chicago Press, 1987.

Morris, William and Mary Morris. *Harper Dictionary of Contemporary Usage.* New York: Harper & Row, 1988.

Sabin, William. *Gregg Reference Manual,* New York: McGraw-Hill, 1989.

U.S. Government Printing Office Style Manual, rev. ed. Washington, DC: Government Printing Office, 1985.

SUGGESTED ANSWERS TO CHAPTER ONE EXERCISES

1. Margaret Duncan must authorize lunch periods longer than one hour fifteen minutes.

2. New employees must present their signed letters of employment for health certification, available through Physician's Medical Center beginning July 15. Only then will they be admitted to the Orientation Course, beginning July 26. Both health certification and orientation must be completed by new employees before they report to their work units, no later than 9 a.m. on August 1.

3. All of us are pleased that you've accepted our job offer.

4. Bob, I'm holding your resignation letter. After seven years of working closely with you, I would like to get together to talk out the issues you raise. Could I ask you to ring my secretary as soon as possible with a time that's good for you?

INDEX